Beyond the Battlefield

14 Scrappy Civil War Quilts

Mary Etherington
and Connie Tesene

Martingale
Create with Confidence

Beyond the Battlefield: 14 Scrappy Civil War Quilts
© 2019 by Mary Etherington and Connie Tesene

Martingale®
19021 120th Ave. NE, Ste. 102
Bothell, WA 98011-9511 USA
ShopMartingale.com

Printed in China
24 23 22 21 20 19   8 7 6 5 4 3 2 1

Library of Congress Cataloging-in-Publication Data is available upon request.

ISBN: 978-1-60468-981-5

MISSION STATEMENT

We empower makers who use fabric and yarn
to make life more enjoyable.

CREDITS

PUBLISHER AND
CHIEF VISIONARY OFFICER
Jennifer Erbe Keltner

CONTENT DIRECTOR
Karen Costello Soltys

MANAGING EDITOR
Tina Cook

ACQUISITIONS EDITOR
Amelia Johanson

TECHNICAL EDITOR
Ellen Pahl

COPY EDITOR
Kathleen Cubley

DESIGN MANAGER
Adrienne Smitke

COVER AND
BOOK DESIGNER
Regina Girard

PHOTOGRAPHER
Brent Kane

ILLUSTRATOR
Sandy Loi

SPECIAL THANKS

*Historical content in this book was provided by
Tanya Tullos, PhD in Educational Curriculum
and Instruction, Texas A&M University.*

*Photography for this book was taken at
Jodi and Lance Allen's home in Woodinville, Washington.*

*Sue Urich of Farmhouse Quilting in Garner, Iowa,
machine quilted several of the quilts in this book.*

CONTENTS

CIRCA 1863
Interior of Fort Sumter

CIRCA 1860-1870
Mary E. Walker

*Dr. Walker volunteered as a surgeon
for the Union army during the Civil War.*

FOREWORD

The Civil War began in South Carolina on April 12, 1861, with the attack on Fort Sumter. In Virginia on April 9, 1865, General Lee surrendered, and the war was considered over. The years between were filled with patriotism, violence, heartbreak, and peril; nothing about the war was very civil. When the war ended, years of pain, resentment, turmoil, and complications were just getting started.

While it's generally accepted that the Civil War involved many thousands of men, both Confederate and Union women took part in the fight as well. Some disguised themselves as men, actually fighting on the battlefields and sometimes being captured or killed. Women also became both doctors and nurses who worked near the action to set up field hospitals and infirmaries. Working as spies for both sides, women received and sent information about troop movements, supply chains, and other vital information. Their daring antics and personal charms became the stuff of legend.

> *Women followed their passions and involved themselves in helping others.*

CIRCA 1865

Frances L. Clalin

Frances disguised herself as a man, "Jack Williams," to fight in the Civil War.

Other women stayed at home as the war came to them. Husbands went away to fight, and in their stead, the women ran businesses, plantations, and families.

As always, women followed their passions and involved themselves in helping others. From 1861 to 1865, intelligent and resourceful women fought, served, organized, wrote, and even died for their beliefs. Their work, bravery, and passion for their causes still inspire us today.

~ *Tanya Tullos, PhD*

Want to learn more about the women portrayed in this book? Visit ShopMartingale.com /BeyondtheBattlefield for a suggested reading list.

SHINING STAR

What a great way for your favorite reproduction prints to shine, in this quilt stitched from 60° triangles.

Materials

Yardage is based on 42"-wide fabric. Fat eighths are 9" × 21".

5 fat eighths of assorted light prints for blocks, sashing, and border

9 fat eighths of assorted pink prints for blocks, sashing, and border

⅜ yard of charcoal print for blocks, sashing, and border

4 fat eighths of assorted black prints for blocks, sashing, and border

1 yard *total* of assorted yellow, teal, and blue prints for sashing and border

⅓ yard of dark print for binding

1⅜ yards of fabric for backing

40" × 46" piece of batting

Template plastic

Cutting

Make A and B templates using patterns on page 10. Measurements include ¼"-wide seam allowances.

From *each* of the 5 light prints, cut:
4 of A and 4 of A reversed (20 total of each)
4 squares, 3½" × 3½" (20 total)

From *each* of the 9 pink prints, cut:
2 of B (18 total)
1 square, 4¼" × 4¼"; cut into quarters diagonally to make 4 triangles (36 total; 18 are extra)

From the charcoal print, cut:
18 of B
5 squares, 4¼" × 4¼"; cut into quarters diagonally to make 20 triangles (2 are extra)

From *each* of the 4 black prints, cut:
4 of A and 4 of A reversed (16 total of each)
4 squares, 3½" × 3½" (16 total)

From the assorted yellow, teal, and blue prints and leftover light, pink, charcoal, and black prints, cut:
118 of B
6 of A and 6 of A reversed

From the dark print binding fabric, cut:
4 strips, 2¼" × 42"

Making the Blocks

Press the seam allowances as indicated by the arrows in the illustrations.

1. For one block, choose eight matching light A triangles, two pink B triangles, two matching pink quarter-square-triangles, two charcoal B triangles, two charcoal quarter-square-triangles, and four matching light 3½" squares.

2. Sew a light A and A reversed to each side of a pink B triangle, matching the dots at the seam intersections. Make two 3½" square pink units and two charcoal units.

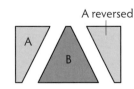
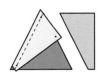

Make 2 of each unit,
3½" × 3½".

CIRCA 1865

Pauline Cushman

Born in 1833 in New Orleans, Harriet Wood dreamed of becoming an actress. In those days, it was a rough life with lots of travel, poor accommodations, little pay, and public disapproval. Despite all of this, Harriet took the name Pauline Cushman and became well known for her stage performances. She sided with the Union when the war began and passed information through a Union network of spies. She escaped capture, and when sentenced to hang, she pleaded illness. President Lincoln made her an honorary cavalry major, and newspapers called her a heroine. She eventually went west, and when Pauline Cushman died in 1893, hundreds of Union veterans attended the service. She was buried with military honors in San Francisco's National Military Cemetery.

3 Sew the charcoal and pink quarter-square-triangles together as shown to make a 3½" square hourglass unit for the block center.

Make 1 unit,
3½" × 3½".

4 Arrange and sew the units from step 2, the hourglass unit, and the four light 3½" squares in three rows as shown. Sew the rows together to make a block measuring 9½" square, including seam allowances. Make five blocks with a light background.

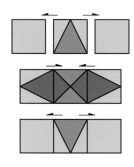 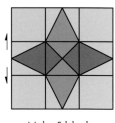

Make 5 blocks,
9½" × 9½".

5 Repeat steps 1–4 using the black A triangles and squares instead of the light print. Make four blocks with a black print background.

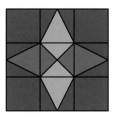

Make 4 blocks,
9½" × 9½".

Making the Sashing and Border

1 Arrange and sew together 17 B triangles, one A triangle, and one A reversed triangle to create a row measuring 3½" × 27½". Make four rows.

Make 4 rows,
3½" × 27½".

Quilt size: 33½" × 39½ " • **Finished block:** 9" × 9"

Shining Star

2 Arrange and sew together 25 B triangles, one A triangle, and one A reversed triangle to create a side border row measuring 3½" × 39½". Make two rows.

Make 2 rows,
3½" × 39½".

Assembling and Finishing the Quilt

1 Arrange and sew the blocks into three rows of three blocks each, alternating the light and dark backgrounds.

2 Referring to the quilt assembly diagram at right, arrange the block rows with the sashing and border rows. Sew the horizontal rows together and then add the side borders. The quilt top should measure 33½" × 39½".

3 Layer the backing, batting, and quilt top. Baste, and then quilt as desired. The quilt shown was machine quilted by Sue Urich with parallel, double horizontal lines.

4 Trim the excess batting and backing. Use the dark print 2¼"-wide strips to bind the quilt.

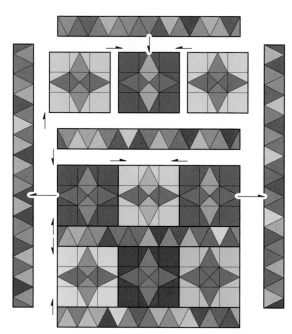

Quilt assembly

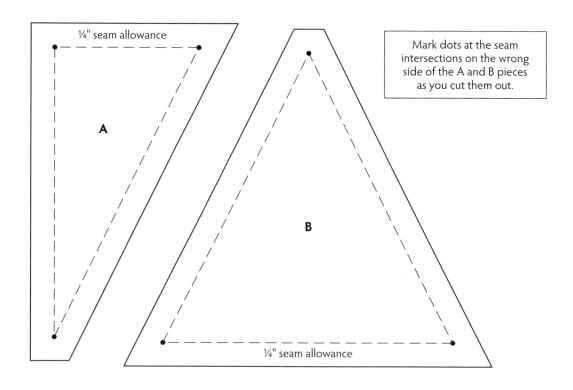

¼" seam allowance

A

B

¼" seam allowance

Mark dots at the seam intersections on the wrong side of the A and B pieces as you cut them out.

CARING HANDS

Traditional Bear's Paw blocks turned this way and that create an interesting formation that keeps your eyes darting across the quilt top.

Materials

Yardage is based on 42"-wide fabric.

1 yard *total* of assorted dark prints in red, blue, brown, gray, and pink for blocks

1¼ yards *total* of assorted light prints for blocks

1½ yards of navy print for setting squares, triangles, and binding

2½ yards of fabric for backing

43" × 60" piece of batting

Cutting

Keep the matching 1⅞" triangles together when cutting. Measurements include ¼"-wide seam allowances.

From assorted dark prints, cut:

96 sets of 2 matching squares, 1⅞" × 1⅞" (192 total); cut in half diagonally to make 4 triangles (384 total)

48 squares, 2⅞" × 2⅞"; cut in half diagonally to make 96 triangles

From assorted light prints, cut:

96 sets of 2 matching squares, 1⅞" × 1⅞" (192 total); cut in half diagonally to make 4 triangles (384 total)

96 squares, 1½" × 1½"

48 squares, 2⅞" × 2⅞"; cut in half diagonally to make 96 triangles

From the navy print, cut:

2 squares, 12½" × 12½"

2 squares, 22" × 22", cut into quarters diagonally to make 8 triangles (2 are extra)

2 squares, 13" × 13", cut in half diagonally to make 4 triangles

5 strips, 2¼" × 42"

Making the Blocks

Press the seam allowances as indicated by the arrows in the illustrations. Each 12" block is made up of 16 block units. Make all of the units and then group them together to make the larger block.

1 Sew four matching light 1⅞" triangles to four matching dark 1⅞" triangles to make four half-square-triangle units measuring 1½" square, including seam allowances.

Make 4 units,
1½" × 1½".

2 Sew a light 2⅞" triangle to a dark 2⅞" triangle to make a half-square-triangle unit measuring 2½" square, including seam allowances.

Make 1 unit,
2½" × 2½".

3 Arrange and sew the units together with a light 1½" square as shown. Make a total of 96 units measuring 3½" square, including seam allowances.

Make 96 units,
3½" × 3½".

CIRCA 1855

Phoebe Pember

Phoebe Pember, a Southern Jewish woman and a childless widow, came from a wealthy family in South Carolina. She was appointed as a hospital administrator and nurse during the Civil War, a position typically held by men. Under her administration, thousands of soldiers were treated in Richmond, Virginia, at what was then the world's largest military hospital. After the war was over, Pember wrote a memoir of her time caring for wounded and dying soldiers.

Quilt size: 37" × 54" • **Finished block:** 12" × 12"

Beyond the Battlefield

4 Arrange and sew 16 of the units into four rows of four units each, rotating them as shown. Sew the rows together to make a block. Make six blocks measuring 12½" square, including seam allowances.

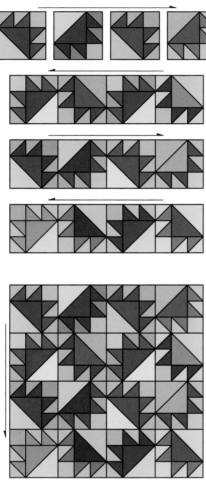

Make 6 blocks,
12½" × 12½".

Assembling and Finishing the Quilt

1 Arrange the six blocks in diagonal rows with the navy 12½" squares and the side and corner setting triangles. Sew the blocks into rows and then sew the rows together. Trim the points of the setting triangles even with the blocks as needed. Add the corner triangles last.

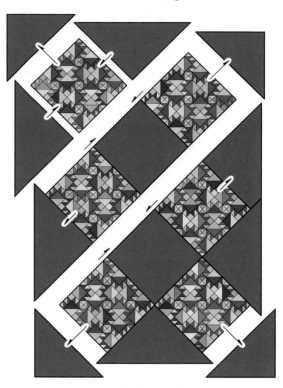

Quilt assembly

2 Trim and square up the quilt top, leaving approximately 1½" beyond the block points. This allows the blocks to "float"; you can trim more or less than 1½", as you prefer. The quilt top should measure approximately 37" × 54".

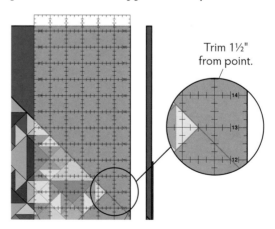

Trim 1½"
from point.

3 Layer the backing, batting, and quilt top. Baste, and then quilt as desired. The quilt shown was machine quilted by Sue Urich in a diagonal grid.

4 Trim the excess batting and backing. Use the navy print 2¼"-wide strips to bind the quilt.

DASHED DREAMS

Can't you just imagine women of the era stitching together bits and pieces to make string-pieced quilts such as this?

Materials

Yardage is based on 42"-wide fabric.

2 yards *total* of assorted scraps for blocks
10" × 10" piece of dark brown print for
    orphan block
⅓ yard of brown print for binding
1⅜ yards of fabric for backing
33" × 47" piece of batting

Cutting

Measurements include ¼"-wide seam allowances.

Cutting the String-Pieced Blocks

From assorted scraps, cut approximately:
240 strips, 1" to 2" × 5½"
95 strips, 1" to 2" × 4½"
75 strips, 1" to 2" × 3½"

Cutting the Orphan Block

From assorted scraps, cut:
15 squares, 1½" × 1½"

From dark brown print, cut:
4 strips, 1½" × 5½"
2 strips, 1½" × 7½"

Cutting the Binding

From the brown print, cut:
4 strips, 2¼" × 42"

Improv Piecing

The opposite of precision piecing is improvisational piecing, and it appears often in modern quilts. The same technique can be used with your favorite Civil War fabrics. This is relaxed sewing at its best.

Gather your scraps and start sewing. Our scraps were assorted widths of 5"-long pieces that we sewed together strip after strip, and then we trimmed blocks to size, either 2½", 3½", or 4½" wide. We also threw in an orphan block. Feel free to substitute a strip-pieced block or other 7½" leftover block for that space.

Making the String-Pieced Blocks

Press the seam allowances as indicated by the arrows in the illustrations. Throughout the steps, cut additional strips if needed.

1 Sew assorted 5½"-long strips together to make a strip that is at least 41" long. Trim the strip to make a block measuring 4½" × 40½".

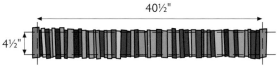

40½"

4½"

Make 1 block.

CIRCA 1860-1870

Varina Howell Davis

Born and raised in Mississippi, Varina Howell Davis married widower Jefferson Davis. When her husband became the Confederate president, Varina Davis took on the role of First Lady. Davis, of course, saw the devastation as the war ravaged the South. As a tribute to the Confederacy, she made a silk quilt that is now in the Museum of the Confederacy in Richmond, Virginia. Davis had many Northern connections and later became good friends with Julia Grant, the wife of Union general Ulysses S. Grant. After Jefferson Davis died in the late 1880s, Varina Davis moved to New York City and worked as a writer.

2 Sew assorted 5½"-long strips together and trim to the dimensions indicated to make the following blocks:
- 1 block, 4½" × 36½"
- 1 block, 4½" × 22½"
- 1 block, 4½" × 20½"
- 1 block, 4½" × 16½"
- 1 block, 4½" × 7½"
- 5 blocks, 4½" × 6½"

3 Sew assorted 4½"-long strips together and trim to the dimensions indicated to make the following blocks:
- 1 block, 3½" × 32½"
- 1 block, 3½" × 22½"
- 1 block, 3½" × 13½"

4 Sew assorted 3½"-long strips together and trim to the dimensions indicated to make the following blocks:
- 1 block, 2½" × 40½"
- 1 block, 2½" × 7½"
- 1 block, 2½" × 6½"

Making the Orphan Block

1 Sew five assorted print 1½" squares together to make a block unit measuring 1½" × 5½". Make three units.

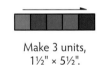

Make 3 units,
1½" × 5½".

2 Arrange and sew the units from step 1 together with the four dark brown print 1½" × 5½" strips. Add the dark brown print 1½" × 7½" strips to the side to make a block measuring 7½" square, including seam allowances.

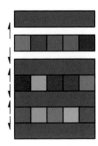 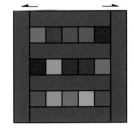

Make 1 block,
7½" × 7½".

Quilt size: 26½" × 40½"

Dashed Dreams

Assembling and Finishing the Quilt

1 Referring to the quilt assembly diagram below, sew the blocks together in sections to complete the quilt top. It should measure 26½" × 40½".

2 Layer the backing, batting, and quilt top. Baste, and then quilt as desired. The quilt shown was machine quilted in parallel horizontal lines at random widths apart.

3 Trim the excess batting and backing. Use the brown print 2¼"-wide strips to bind the quilt.

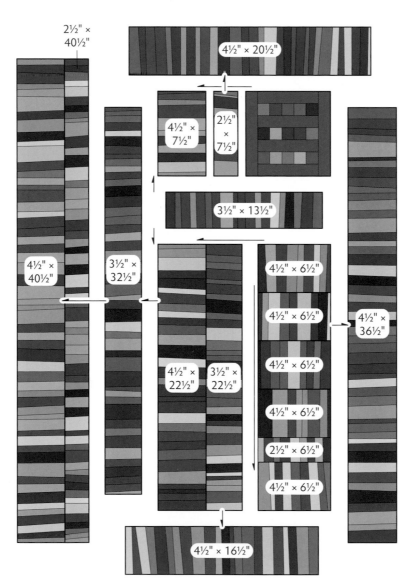

Quilt assembly

A LABOR OF LOVE

Petite Cake Stand blocks work effortlessly together in this design. Baptist fan quilting completes the look, which is so apropos for the era.

Materials

Yardage is based on 42"-wide fabric.

42 squares, 5" × 5", of assorted light prints for blocks
84 squares, 6" × 6", of assorted medium to dark prints for blocks
⅜ yard of light blue print for setting blocks
⅜ yard of red print for setting triangles
⅜ yard of brown stripe for border
⅓ yard of brown print for binding
1 yard of fabric for backing
34" × 38" piece of batting

Cutting

Measurements include ¼"-wide seam allowances.

Cutting 1 Block

Cut 42 total.

From a light print square, cut:
2 squares, 1⅝" × 1⅝"; cut in half diagonally to make 4 triangles
1 square, 1¼" × 1¼"
2 rectangles, 1¼" × 2"

From *1* medium or dark print, cut:
3 squares, 1⅝" × 1⅝"; cut in half diagonally to make 6 triangles
1 square, 2⅜" × 2⅜"; cut in half diagonally to make 2 triangles (1 is extra)

From a second medium or dark print, cut:
1 square, 2⅜" × 2⅜"; cut in half diagonally to make 2 triangles

Cutting the Remainder of the Quilt

From the light blue print, cut:
3 strips, 3½" × 42"; crosscut into 30 squares, 3½" × 3½"

From the red print, cut:
6 squares, 6" × 6"; cut into quarters diagonally to make 24 triangles (2 are extra)
2 squares, 4" × 4"; cut in half diagonally to make 4 triangles

From the brown stripe, cut:
2 strips, 2½" × 26"
2 strips, 2½" × 34¼"

From the brown print, cut:
4 strips, 2¼" × 42"

Making the Blocks

Press the seam allowances as indicated by the arrows in the illustrations.

1   Sew a light 1⅝" triangle to a medium or dark 1⅝" triangle to make a half-square-triangle unit measuring 1¼" square. Make four units.

Make 4 units,
1¼" × 1¼".

2   Sew a medium or dark 2⅜" triangle to the second medium or dark 2⅜" triangle to make a half-square-triangle unit measuring 2" square.

Make 1 unit,
2" × 2".

3   Sew a medium or dark 1⅝" triangle to each light 1¼" × 2" rectangle as shown.

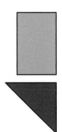 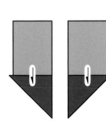

Make 1 of each unit.

4   Arrange and sew the units together as shown with the light 1¼" square and the remaining second medium or dark 2⅜" triangle. The block should measure 3½" square, including

CIRCA 1860-1875

Vinnie Ream

Vinnie Ream was born in Madison, Wisconsin, in 1847, and in 1861, her family moved to Washington, D.C. It must have seemed like a city of dreams and light for the young girl. At age 14, she was among the first females hired to work at the United States Postal Service. Ream's real gift, however, was working with clay. She took classes and apprenticed with a noted sculptor. Determined and talented, Ream overcame obstacles to work as a "woman artist." When Ream was still a teen, President Lincoln agreed to model for her so that she could create his likeness. After his assassination, Vinnie Ream was commissioned by Congress to sculpt the life-sized statue of Abraham Lincoln that is today in the Capitol Rotunda.

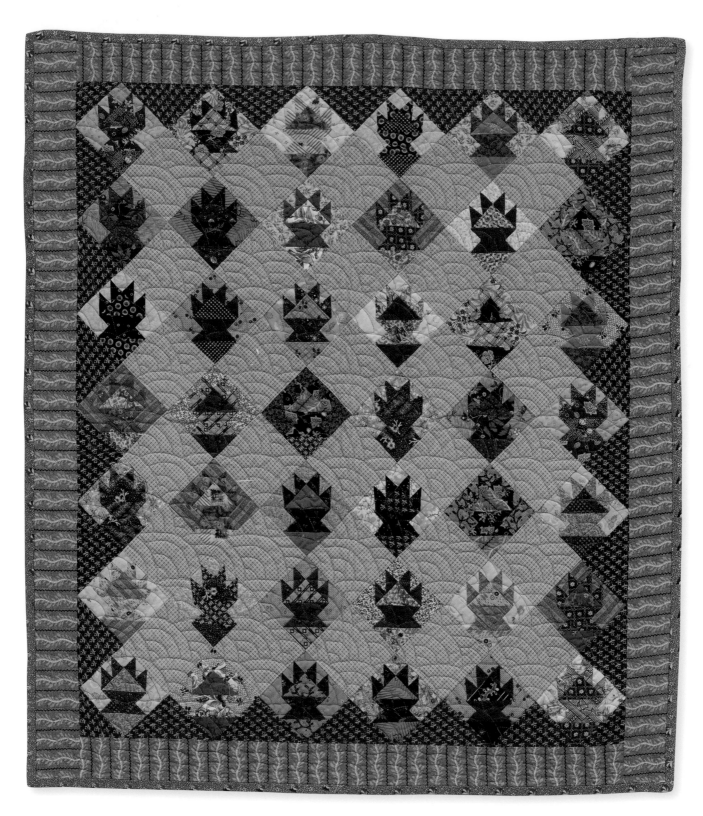

Quilt size: 30" × 34¼" • **Finished block:** 3" × 3"

seam allowances. Make a total of 42 Cake Stand blocks.

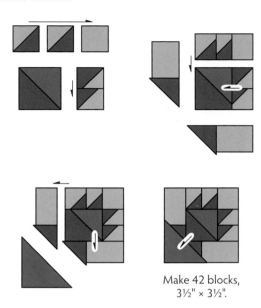

Make 42 blocks,
3½" × 3½".

Assembling and Finishing the Quilt

1 Arrange and sew the blocks, light blue 3½" squares, and the red print triangles in diagonal rows. Sew the rows together and add the corner triangles.

2 Trim and square up the quilt center to measure 26" × 30¼", making sure there is at least ¼" seam allowance beyond the points of the blocks.

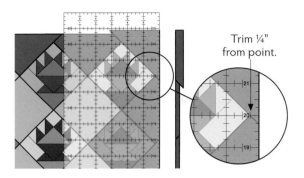

Trim ¼" from point.

3 Sew a brown stripe 2½" × 26" border strip to the top and bottom of the quilt. Sew a brown stripe 2½" × 34¼" border to each side.

4 Layer the backing, batting, and quilt top. Baste, and then quilt as desired. The quilt shown was machine quilted in an overall Baptist fan design.

5 Trim the excess batting and backing. Use the brown print 2¼"-wide strips to bind the quilt.

Quilt assembly

A Labor of Love

Heartbeats

Clara Barton notably started the American Red Cross. The cross, a familiar motif to quilters, is replicated here, framed in blue and gray.

Materials

Yardage is based on 42"-wide fabric.

9 scraps, 5" × 5", of assorted red prints for blocks
9 scraps, 5" × 5", of assorted light prints for blocks
5 scraps, 5" × 10", of assorted navy prints for blocks
4 scraps, 5" × 10", of assorted gray prints for blocks
¼ yard of light print for sashing
⅛ yard of gold print #1 for sashing stars
6" × 10" scrap of gold print #2 for border
¼ yard of red print for border
5" × 5" scrap of navy print for border
¼ yard of navy print for binding
¾ yard of fabric for backing
26" × 26" piece of batting

Cutting

Measurements include ¼"-wide seam allowances.

From *each* red scrap, cut:
1 rectangle, 1½" × 3½" (9 total)
2 squares, 1½" × 1½" (18 total)

From *each* light scrap, cut:
4 squares, 1½" × 1½" (36 total)

From *each* of the navy or gray print scraps, cut:
2 rectangles, 1½" × 3½" (18 total)
2 rectangles, 1½" × 5½" (18 total)

From the light print, cut:
1 strip, 5½" × 42"; crosscut into 12 rectangles,
   2" × 5½"

From gold print #1, cut:
1 strip, 1¼" × 42"; crosscut into 32 squares, 1¼" × 1¼"
4 squares, 2" × 2"

From the red print, cut:
1 strip, 5½" × 42"; crosscut into 12 rectangles,
   2" × 5½"

From gold print #2, cut:
8 squares, 2" × 2"

From the navy 5" scrap, cut:
4 squares, 2" × 2"

From navy print for binding, cut:
3 strips, 2¼" × 42"

Making the Blocks

Press the seam allowances as indicated by the arrows in the illustrations.

1 Arrange and sew two red print 1½" squares, a red print 1½" × 3½" rectangle, and four light print 1½" squares together in rows. Sew the rows together to make a cross unit measuring 3½" square.

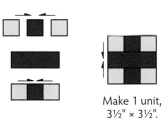

Make 1 unit,
3½" × 3½".

CIRCA 1866

Clara Barton

Nurse Clara Barton helped anyone who was hurting—she tended wounded and dying men of both the North and South during the Civil War and was nicknamed the Angel of the Battlefield. Soldiers later recalled the heroics of Nurse Barton treating them amid danger. Barton also helped after the horrific Johnstown, Pennsylvania, flood. She took supplies to Cuba after the explosion of the battleship *Maine* in 1898, and she helped after the great storm in Galveston, Texas, in 1900 when she was in her late 70s. In these and other places, Barton collected, organized, and distributed medical supplies and used her administrative skills to help make nursing safer and more professional. In a lasting legacy, she founded the American Red Cross to assist in times of disaster.

2 Sew two navy 1½" × 3½" rectangles to opposite sides of the cross unit. Sew two navy 1½" × 5½" rectangles to the top and bottom to make a block measuring 5½" square, including seam allowances. Make five blocks.

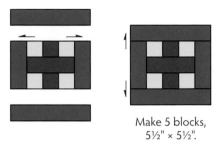

Make 5 blocks,
5½" × 5½".

3 Repeat steps 1 and 2 to make four blocks with gray rectangles.

Make 4 blocks,
5½" × 5½".

Making the Sashing and Borders

1 Draw a diagonal line from corner to corner on the wrong side of the gold print 1¼" squares. Place a marked square on one corner of a light print 2" × 5½" rectangle and sew on the line. Trim the outside corner of the square only, ¼" from the stitched line. Repeat on the adjacent corner to make a sashing unit measuring 2" × 5½". Make eight units with triangles on two corners.

Make 8 units,
2" × 5½".

Quilt size: 21½" × 21½" • **Finished block:** 5" × 5"

2 Repeat step 1 to make four units with triangles on all four corners.

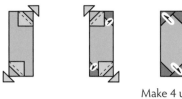

Make 4 units,
2" × 5½".

3 Sew three of the units together with two 2" gold print #1 squares as shown to make a sashing row measuring 2" × 18½". Make two rows.

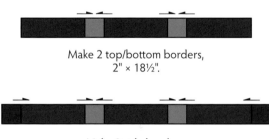

Make 2 rows,
2" × 18½".

4 Sew three red print 2" × 5½" rectangles together with two gold print #2 squares to make a top/bottom border measuring 2" × 18½". Make two. Make two side borders in the same manner, adding a navy 2" square to each end. The side borders should measure 2" × 21½".

Make 2 top/bottom borders,
2" × 18½".

Make 2 side borders,
2" × 21½".

Assembling and Finishing the Quilt

1 Arrange the blocks, remaining sashing units, and the sashing rows together. Sew the blocks and sashing strips into rows and then join the block rows and sashing rows to make a quilt center measuring 18½" square, including seam allowances.

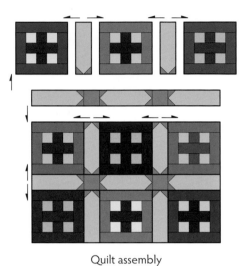

Quilt assembly

2 Sew the borders to the top and bottom of the quilt and then to each side. The quilt top should now measure 21½" square.

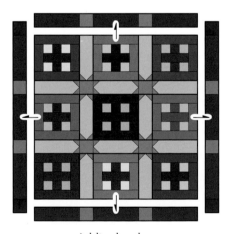

Adding borders

3 Layer the backing, batting, and quilt top. Baste, and then quilt as desired. The quilt shown was machine quilted in parallel horizontal lines.

4 Trim the excess batting and backing. Use the navy print 2¼"-wide strips to bind the quilt.

VANISHING CIRCLES

If you've never read Little Women *(or even if you have), imagine stitching this quilt while sitting before the fire and listening to the audio book.*

Materials

Yardage is based on 42"-wide fabric.

4" × 10" scrap of green print for center Star block

½ yard *total* of assorted red prints for center Star block, red Star blocks, and center appliqué blocks

1⅜ yards *total* of assorted light to medium prints for Star blocks and appliqué blocks

¼ yard *total* of assorted blue and navy prints for blue Star blocks

⅞ yard *total* of assorted dark prints for appliqué blocks

⅓ yard of pink print for setting squares

½ yard of navy print #1 for setting squares

¼ yard *each* of 2 blue prints for setting triangles

½ yard of navy print #2 for binding

3 yards of fabric for backing

52" × 52" piece of batting

Supplies for your preferred method of appliqué

Cutting

Measurements include ¼"-wide seam allowances.

Cutting the Center Star Block

From the green scrap, cut:
12 squares, 1½" × 1½"

From a red print, cut:
1 square, 2½" × 2½"

From the assorted light to medium prints, cut:
4 matching rectangles, 1½" × 2½"
4 matching squares, 1½" × 1½"

Cutting 1 Blue Star Block

Cut 8 blocks total.

From assorted light to medium prints, cut:
2 matching squares, 1½" × 1½"
4 matching rectangles, 1½" × 2½"
4 matching squares, 1½" × 1½"

Continued on page 33

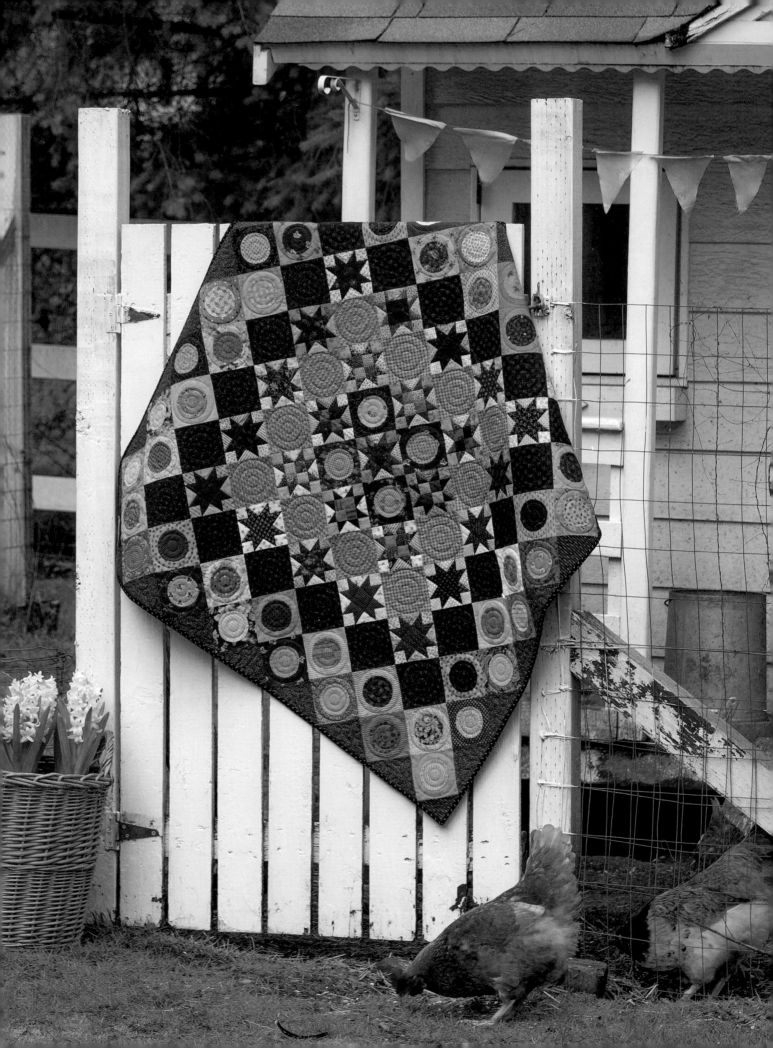

Continued from page 31

From assorted blue and navy prints, cut:
2 matching squares, 1½" × 1½"
8 matching squares, 1½" × 1½"

Cutting 1 Red Star Block

Cut 16 blocks total.

From assorted light prints, cut:
4 matching rectangles, 1½" × 2½"
4 matching squares, 1½" × 1½"

From assorted red prints, cut:
1 square, 2½" × 2½"
8 matching squares, 1½" × 1½"

Cutting the Appliqué Blocks

Use the circle pattern on page 36.

From assorted red prints, cut:
4 squares, 4½" × 4½"

From assorted light to medium prints, cut:
32 circles
24 squares, 4½" × 4½"

From assorted dark prints, cut:
24 circles
28 squares, 4½" × 4½"

Cutting the Remainder of the Quilt

From the pink print, cut:
2 strips, 4½" × 42"; crosscut into 12 squares,
   4½" × 4½"

From navy print #1, cut:
3 strips, 4½" × 42"; crosscut into 20 squares,
   4½" × 4½"

**From the blue prints for setting triangles, cut
a total of:**
7 squares, 7½" × 7½"; cut into quarters diagonally
   to yield 28 triangles
2 squares, 4½" × 4½"; cut in half diagonally to yield
   4 triangles

From navy print #2, cut:
5 strips, 2¼" × 42"

CIRCA 1870

Louisa May Alcott

During the Civil War, Louisa May Alcott worked as a nurse in Washington, D.C. When she contracted typhoid fever, she went home to Concord, Massachusetts, to recover. Unfortunately, the medicine with which she was treated contained mercury, and she suffered from mercury poisoning for the rest of her life. Alcott wrote a book about her experiences, *Hospital Sketches*, based on her work as a nurse. Alcott is probably best known as the author of *Little Women*, one of the most loved novels about a family during the Civil War period.

Quilt size: 45¾" × 45¾" • **Finished block:** 4" × 4"

Making the Center Star Block

Press all seam allowances as indicated by the arrows in the illustrations.

1 Draw a diagonal line from corner to corner on the wrong side of the 12 green print 1½" squares. Place a marked square on opposite corners of the red print 2½" square. Sew on the drawn line and trim the outside corner of the square only, ¼" from the stitched line. Repeat on the remaining corners to make the block center.

Make 1 unit,
2½" × 2½".

2 Place a marked square on the corner of a light print 1½" × 2½" rectangle. Sew, trim, and press as in step 1. Repeat on the opposite corner to make a flying-geese unit. Make four units.

Make 4 units,
1½" × 2½".

3 Arrange and sew the units from steps 1 and 2 and the light print 1½" squares in rows as shown. Sew the rows together to complete the center Star block. It should measure 4½" square, including seam allowances.

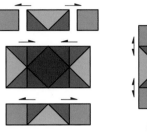 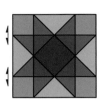

Make 1 block,
4½" × 4½".

Making the Blue Star Blocks

1 Draw a diagonal line from corner to corner on the wrong side of eight blue 1½" squares. Sew the marked squares to a light 1½" × 2½" rectangle, as you did for the center Star block, to make a flying-geese unit. Make four units measuring 1½" × 2½", including seam allowances.

Make 4 units,
1½" × 2½".

2 Sew the two light print and blue print 1½" squares together as shown to make a four-patch unit for the block center. It should measure 2½" square, including seam allowances.

Make 1 unit,
2½" × 2½".

3 Arrange and sew the units from steps 1 and 2 and the light print 1½" squares in rows as shown. Sew the rows together to complete a blue Star block. Make eight blocks, measuring 4½" square, including seam allowances.

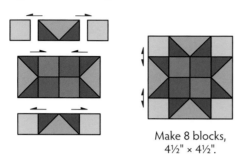

Make 8 blocks,
4½" × 4½".

Making the Red Star Blocks

1 Make four flying-geese units using eight red 1½" squares and four light 1½" × 2½" rectangles. The units should measure 1½" × 2½", including seam allowances.

Make 4 units,
1½" × 2½".

2 Arrange and sew the units from step 1, the light print 1½" squares, and the red 2½" square in rows as shown. Sew the rows together to complete a red Star block. Make 16 blocks, measuring 4½" square, including seam allowances.

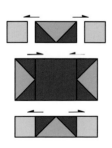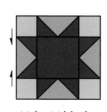

Make 16 blocks,
4½" × 4½".

Making the Appliqué Blocks

1 Using your favorite appliqué method, prepare a circle for appliqué.

2 Choose a 4½" square that contrasts in value so that the circle stands out nicely. Fold the square in half and then in quarters to mark the center. Position the appliqué on the square so that it is centered and stitch it in place by hand or machine. Make a total of 24 blocks with a light background and 32 blocks with a dark background.

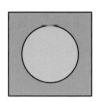

Make 24 blocks,   Make 32 blocks,
4½" × 4½".   4½" × 4½".

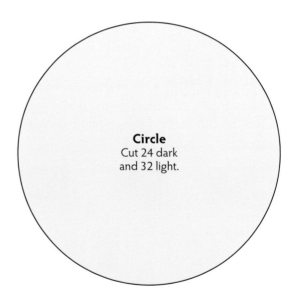

Circle
Cut 24 dark
and 32 light.

Pattern does not include
seam allowance.

Assembling and Finishing the Quilt

1 Following the quilt assembly diagram below, arrange the center Star block, the red and blue Star blocks, the appliquéd circle blocks, the pink squares, and navy squares in diagonal rows. Add the navy side and corner setting triangles. Note that the triangles were cut oversized and will be trimmed after assembly.

2 When you are happy with the placement, sew the blocks, squares, and side triangles into rows. Join the rows and add the corner triangles.

3 Trim the oversized triangles all around, leaving a ¼" seam allowance beyond the block corners.

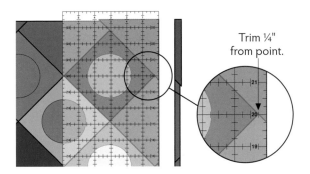

Trim ¼"
from point.

4 Layer the backing, batting, and quilt top. Baste, and then quilt as desired. The quilt shown was machine quilted by Sue Urich with concentric circles in the setting squares and appliquéd blocks. The star blocks were quilted in the ditch.

5 Trim the excess batting and backing. Use the navy print 2¼"-wide strips to bind the quilt.

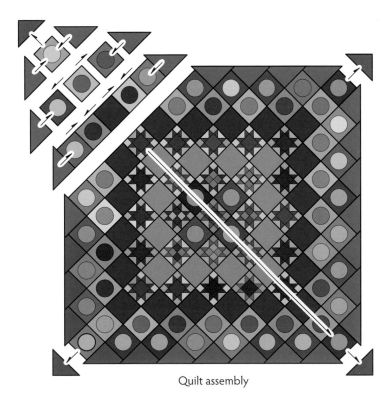

Quilt assembly

FREEDOM, OH, FREEDOM

This charming graphic quilt resembles an old-fashioned game board and a complicated route to freedom.

Materials

Yardage is based on 42"-wide fabric. Fat quarters are 18" × 21".

½ yard *total* of assorted dark prints in teal, tan, brown, black, and gray for blocks
⅝ yard *total* of assorted red prints for blocks, appliqués, and border
⅝ yard *total* of assorted light prints for blocks
⅜ yard of black print for inner borders
2 fat quarters of different light prints for appliqué border
⅓ yard of red print for binding
1⅛ yards of fabric for backing
37" × 37" piece of batting
Template plastic or freezer paper

Cutting

Measurements include ¼"-wide seam allowances. Make a template from the appliqué pattern (page 43) and prepare the pieces for your favorite appliqué method.

From assorted dark and assorted red prints, cut:
18 squares, 2⅞" × 2⅞"; cut in half diagonally to make 36 triangles
28 sets of 2 matching squares, 2⅞" × 2⅞" (56 total); cut in half diagonally to make 4 triangles (112 total)

From assorted light prints, cut:
18 squares, 2⅞" × 2⅞"; cut in half diagonally to make 36 triangles
28 sets of 2 matching squares, 2⅞" × 2⅞" (56 total); cut in half diagonally to make 4 triangles (112 total)

From the black print, cut:
2 strips, 1½" × 24½"
2 strips, 1½" × 22½"
2 strips, 1½" × 14½"
2 strips, 1½" × 12½"

From *each* of the light print fat quarters, cut:
2 rectangles, 4½" × 14½" (4 total)

From the *remainder* of the assorted red prints, cut:
24 appliqué shapes

From *1* of the red prints, cut:
4 squares, 4½" × 4½"

From the red print for binding, cut:
4 strips, 2¼" × 42"

Making the Blocks

Press the seam allowances as indicated by the arrows in the illustrations.

1 Pair an assorted light and dark 2⅞" triangle and sew together to make a half-square-triangle unit measuring 2½" square, including seam allowances. Make 36 units.

Make 36 units,
2½" × 2½".

CIRCA 1893

Harriet Beecher Stowe

Harriet Beecher Stowe grew up in
Connecticut as the daughter of a
minister. She is best known for writing *Uncle
Tom's Cabin,* a novel that depicted the horrors
of slavery. The book was published first in
weekly newspaper installments and again in
1852 as a best-selling book. Many Southerners
felt that it portrayed all masters as villains
like Simon Legree, but the book moved many
in the North to join in antislavery work. The
stage was set for people to make their own
decisions about slavery, and few could look
away from the coming crisis in the nation.
For the rest of her life, Stowe wrote books
and articles and spoke out for equality and
freedom for all people.

2 Sew four of the half-square-triangle units
together as shown to make a Pinwheel block
measuring 4½" square, including seam
allowances. Make nine scrappy blocks for the
quilt center.

Make 9 blocks,
4½" × 4½".

3 Repeat step 1 using four matching light and
four matching dark triangles to make four half-
square-triangle units measuring 2½" square.

4 Sew the four matching units together as shown
to make a Pinwheel block measuring 4½"
square, including seam allowances. Make 28
blocks for the border.

Make 28 blocks,
4½" × 4½".

Appliquéing the Borders

Position and appliqué six shapes to a light print
4½" × 14½" rectangle, aligning the raw edges of the
appliqués with the edge of the rectangle. Make four
appliquéd borders.

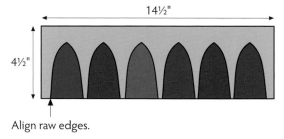

Make 4 borders.

Quilt size: 32½" × 32½" • **Finished block:** 4" × 4"

Freedom, Oh, Freedom

3 Sew an appliquéd border to the top and bottom of the quilt center. Sew a red print square to each end of the remaining two appliquéd borders and then sew one border to each side. The quilt center should measure 22½" square, including seam allowances.

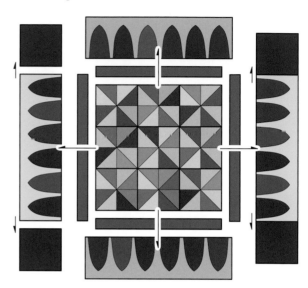

Quilt assembly

Assembling and Finishing the Quilt

1 Arrange and sew the nine scrappy Pinwheel blocks together in three rows of three blocks each to create a quilt center measuring 12½" square, including seam allowances.

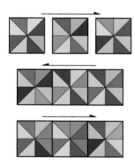 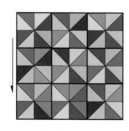

Quilt center,
12½" × 12½"

2 Sew a black print 1½" × 12½" strip to the top and bottom of the quilt center. Sew a black print 1½" × 14½" strip to each side. The quilt center should measure 14½" square, including seam allowances.

4 Sew a black print 1½" × 22½" border to each side of the quilt center. Sew a black print 1½" × 24½" border strip to the top and bottom. The quilt center should measure 24½" square, including seam allowances.

5 Sew six of the Pinwheel blocks together to make the top and bottom borders. Make two. Sew eight of the Pinwheel blocks together to make a side border. Repeat to make two.

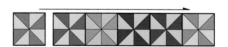

Make 2 top/bottom borders,
4½" × 24½".

Make 2 side borders,
4½" × 32½".

6 Sew the pinwheel borders to the top and bottom of the quilt and then to each side. The quilt top should measure 32½" square.

Adding borders

7 Layer the backing, batting, and quilt top. Baste, and then quilt as desired. The quilt shown was machine quilted by Sue Urich with a diagonal grid in the Pinwheel blocks and arcs in and around the appliqués.

8 Trim the excess batting and backing. Use the red print 2¼"-wide strips to bind the quilt.

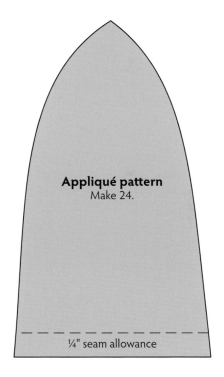

Appliqué pattern
Make 24.

¼" seam allowance

Curved edges of appliqué pattern do not include seam allowances.

Freedom, Oh, Freedom
≈ 43 ≈

Same Tune, New Verse

Nine Patches big and small are combined in a dynamic setting suitable for a tribute to lyricist Julia Ward Howe.

❊

Materials

Yardage is based on 42"-wide fabric. Fat quarters are 18" × 21" and fat eighths are 9" × 21".

16 strips, 2½" × 15", of assorted navy and dark brown prints for large nine-patch units

16 strips, 2½" × 12", of assorted medium blue and brown prints for large nine-patch units

1⅜ yards *total* of assorted red prints for small nine-patch and half-square-triangle units

1¼ yards *total* of assorted light prints for small nine-patch and half-square-triangle units

16 scraps, 4" × 7", of assorted light blue and brown prints for blocks

16 fat quarters of assorted light to medium blue and brown prints for blocks

16 fat eighths of assorted navy and dark brown prints for blocks

⅝ yard of red stripe for block corners

⅔ yard of navy print for border

⅝ yard of fabric for binding*

4⅓ yards of fabric for backing

77" × 77" piece of batting

The quilt shown has a binding made of scraps.

Cutting

Measurements include ¼"-wide seam allowances.

From *each* navy and dark brown strip, cut:
5 squares, 2½" × 2½" (80 total)

From *each* medium blue and brown strip, cut:
4 squares, 2½" × 2½" (64 total)

From assorted red prints, cut:
96 squares, 2⅞" × 2⅞"; cut in half diagonally to make 192 triangles
50 sets of 5 matching squares, 1½" × 1½" (250 total)

From assorted light prints, cut:
96 squares, 2⅞" × 2⅞", cut in half diagonally to make 192 triangles
50 sets of 4 matching squares, 1½" × 1½" (200 total)

From *each* light blue and light brown scrap, cut:
2 squares, 2⅞" × 2⅞" (32 total); cut in half diagonally to make 4 triangles (64 total)

From *each* navy and dark brown fat eighth, cut:
4 rectangles, 3½" × 6½" (64 total)
2 squares, 2⅞" × 2⅞" (32 total); cut in half diagonally to make 4 triangles (64 total)

From *each* light blue and light brown fat quarter, cut:
8 squares, 3½" × 3½" (128 total)
8 rectangles, 2½" × 3½" (128 total)

From red stripe, cut:
5 strips, 3½" × 42"; crosscut into 50 squares, 3½" × 3½"

From navy print, cut:
6 strips, 3½" × 42"; crosscut into 16 rectangles, 3½" × 10½"

From binding fabric, cut:
8 strips, 2¼" × 42"*

For a scrappy binding, cut enough 2¼"-wide strips to make a binding that is at least 294" long.

Julia Ward Howe

Julia Ward Howe, born in 1819 in New York City, wrote books and poems, and she and her husband edited an abolitionist newspaper. On a trip to the White House, the couple actually saw fighting, and Howe was challenged to write more appropriate words for the popular marching tune "John Brown's Body." Her poem "The Battle Hymn of the Republic" earned $5 when The Atlantic Monthly published it in February of 1862. The song is one of the most popular and well-known songs of the Civil War era and made Howe famous. It was later adopted by the women's movement and often used in civil rights efforts.

Making the Large Nine-Patch Units

Press all seam allowances as indicated by the arrows in the illustrations. To simplify block construction, the instructions are written for making all of the nine-patch units and the scrappy half-square-triangle units before assembling the blocks.

Arrange and sew five matching navy or dark brown 2½" squares and four matching medium blue or brown 2½" squares into three rows of three squares each. Join the rows to make a nine-patch unit measuring 6½" square, including seam allowances. Make 16 units.

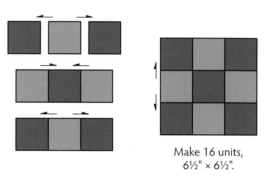

Make 16 units,
6½" × 6½".

Making the Small Nine-Patch Units

Arrange and sew five matching red 1½" squares and four matching light 1½" squares into three rows of three squares each. Join the rows to make a unit measuring 3½" square, including seam allowances. Make a total of 50 nine-patch units. You will use 32 of the units in the blocks and 18 in the pieced border.

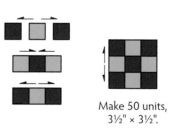

Make 50 units,
3½" × 3½".

Quilt size: 70½" × 70½" • **Finished block:** 16" × 16"

Making the Red and Light Half-Square-Triangle Units

Sew a light 2⅞" triangle together with a red print 2⅞" triangle to make a half-square-triangle unit measuring 2½" square, including seam allowances. Make a total of 192 units.

Make 192 units, 2½" × 2½".

Making the Blocks

Press the seam allowances as indicated by the arrows in the illustrations.

For each block, you will need the following units and pieces:

- 1 medium and dark 6½" nine-patch unit
- 2 red and light 3½" nine-patch units
- 12 assorted red and light 2½" half-square-triangle units
- 1 set of 8 matching light blue or light brown 2½" × 3½" rectangles and 8 matching 3½" squares
- 1 set of 4 matching navy or dark brown 3½" × 6½" rectangles and 4 matching 2⅞" triangles
- 1 set of 4 matching light blue or light brown 2⅞" triangles
- 2 red stripe 3½" squares

1. Sew a light blue or light brown 2⅞" triangle to a navy or dark brown 2⅞" triangle to make a half-square-triangle unit measuring 2½" square. Make four units. Note that some of the blocks use light brown or blue 2⅞" squares that match the other light brown or blue fabric. Mix or match from block to block as desired.

Make 4 units, 2½" × 2½".

2. Draw a diagonal line from corner to corner on the wrong side of the light blue or light brown

3½" squares. Layer a marked square right sides together with the navy or dark brown 3½" × 6½" rectangle as shown. Sew on the line, trim the seam allowance to ¼", and press. Repeat on the opposite end of the rectangle to make a flying-geese unit measuring 3½" × 6½". Make four units.

Make 4 units, 3½" × 6½".

3. Sew a matching light blue or light brown 2½" × 3½" rectangle to each of the units from step 2 to make a unit measuring 3½" × 10½", including seam allowances. Make four units.

Make 4 units, 3½" × 10½".

4. Arrange the four half-square-triangle units from step 1 and the 12 red-and-light half-square-triangle units around the large nine-patch unit as shown. Make sure the half-square-triangle units are oriented correctly and the step 1 units are in what will be the corners of the block. Sew them together in groups of five for the sides and three for the top and bottom. Sew the units to the nine-patch block center to make a unit measuring 10½" square, including seam allowances.

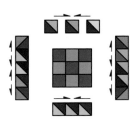 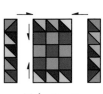

Make 1 unit, 10½" × 10½".

5 Arrange and sew the units from step 3, two small nine-patch units, the red stripe 3½" squares, and the block center unit in three rows as shown. Sew the rows together to complete a block measuring 16½" square, including seam allowances. Make a total of 16 blocks.

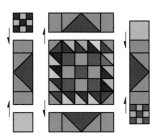 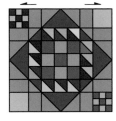

Make 16 blocks,
16½" × 16½".

Assembling and Finishing the Quilt

1 Arrange and sew the blocks in four rows of four blocks each. Join the rows to make a quilt center measuring 64½" square.

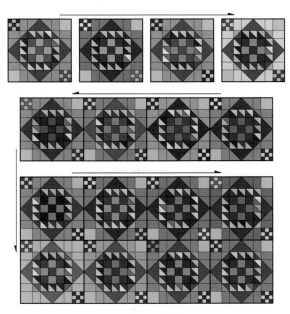

Quilt assembly

2 Sew a pieced border for the top and bottom using four navy print 3½" × 10½" rectangles, four 3½" nine-patch units, and four red stripe

3½" squares. Make two borders measuring 3½" × 64½". Repeat for the side borders, adding another nine-patch unit and red stripe square at each end to make two borders measuring 3½" × 70½".

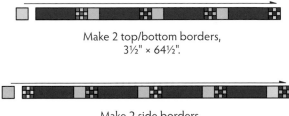

Make 2 top/bottom borders,
3½" × 64½".

Make 2 side borders,
3½" × 70½".

3 Add the top and bottom borders to the quilt center. Add the side borders. The quilt top should now measure 70½" square.

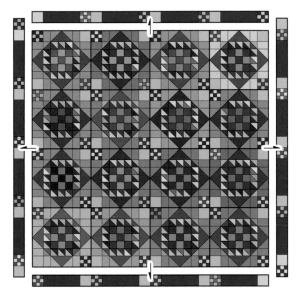

Adding borders

4 Layer the backing, batting, and quilt top. Baste, and then quilt as desired. The quilt shown was machine quilted by Calico Hutch in an overall meandering design.

5 Trim the excess batting and backing. Use the dark print (or scrappy) 2¼"-wide strips to bind the quilt.

It's easy to create the illusion of a medallion setting simply by rotating blocks with strong diagonal components.

Quilt size: 30½" × 30½" • **Finished block:** 3" × 3"

Materials

Yardage is based on 42"-wide fabric. Fat quarters measure 18" × 21".

1¼ yards *total* of assorted light prints for Star blocks and Jacob's Ladder blocks

¾ yard *total* of assorted medium or dark prints in black, navy, teal, gold, pink, red, rust, and brown for Star blocks

¼ yard *total* of assorted red prints for Jacob's Ladder blocks

¼ yard *total* of assorted gray prints for Jacob's Ladder blocks

⅓ yard of blue print for binding

1 yard of fabric for backing

35" × 35" piece of batting

Cutting

Measurements include ¼"-wide seam allowances.

From assorted light prints, cut:
52 squares, 2" × 2"*
52 sets of 8 matching squares, 1¼" × 1¼"
96 pairs of matching squares, 1¼" × 1¼"
48 squares, 2⅜" × 2⅜"

From assorted medium to dark prints, cut:
52 sets of 4 matching rectangles, 1¼" × 2" and 4 squares, 1¼" × 1¼"

From the assorted red prints, cut:
48 sets of 4 matching squares, 1¼" × 1¼"

From the assorted gray prints, cut:
48 squares, 2⅜" × 2⅜"

From the blue print, cut:
4 strips, 2¼" × 42"

Some of the Star blocks use only one light print. For these, cut one 2" square for the star center from the same fabric as the eight matching 1¼" squares.

Making the Star Blocks

Press the seam allowances as indicated by the arrows in the illustrations. Use one or two light prints and one dark print for each block. You will need the following pieces for one block:

- 1 light 2" square
- 8 matching light 1¼" squares
- 1 set of 4 matching dark rectangles, 1¼" × 2", and 4 squares, 1¼" × 1¼"

1 Draw a diagonal line on the wrong side of each light 1¼" square. Place a marked square on a dark 1¼" × 2" rectangle, right sides together. Sew on the drawn line and trim the outside corner of the square only, ¼" from the stitched line. Repeat on the other end of the rectangle. Make four units.

Make 4 units,
1¼" × 2".

Sarah Emma Edmonds

A Canadian by birth, Sarah Emma Edmonds left home and came to America to escape an early marriage. She disguised herself as a man named Frank Thompson and enlisted in the Union army, where she fought and worked as a male nurse and spy. In 1863, she left the Union army. Some think that she needed medical treatment for malaria and was afraid her gender would be revealed. Since Frank Thompson was listed as a deserter, Edmonds worked as a female nurse under her own name. She went on to marry and have a family. Charges of desertion were later dropped and Edmonds received a soldier's pension of $12 a month for her Union loyalty and service.

2 Arrange and sew the units from step 1, the four dark 1¼" squares, and the light 2" square in rows as shown. Join the rows to make a Star block measuring 3½" square, including seam allowances. Make 52 blocks.

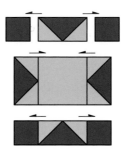 

Make 52 blocks,
3½" × 3½".

Taming of the Scraps

My love of scrap quilts comes with the troublesome issue of "taming" the fabric. I use empty shoeboxes to stay organized. I place all scraps with the same measurement into a marked box with "like-minded" strips. It makes cutting a scrap quilt just a little easier . . . and my shoeboxes are put to good use!

~ Connie

Making the Jacob's Ladder Block

For each block, you will need the following pieces:
- 4 matching light 1¼" squares
- 4 matching red 1¼" squares
- 2 matching gray print 2⅜" triangles
- 2 matching light print 2⅜" triangles

1 Sew two matching red and two matching light 1¼" squares together to make a four-patch unit measuring 2" square. Make two units.

Make 2 units,
2" × 2".

2 Sew a light triangle to a gray triangle to make a half-square-triangle unit measuring 2" square. Make two units.

Make 2 units,
2" × 2".

3 Arrange and sew the four-patch units and half-square-triangle units together as shown to complete a Jacob's Ladder block measuring 3½" square, including seam allowances. Make a total of 48 blocks.

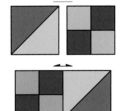 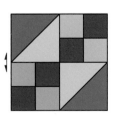

Make 48 blocks,
3½" × 3½".

Assembling and Finishing the Quilt

1 Arrange the Star blocks and Jacob's Ladder blocks on a design wall or your floor in 10 rows of 10 blocks each, alternating them as shown. Once you are satisfied with the color placement, sew the blocks together in rows. Join the rows to complete a quilt top measuring 30½" square.

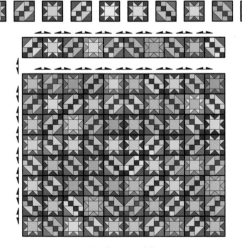

Quilt assembly

2 Layer the backing, batting, and quilt top. Baste, and then quilt as desired. The quilt shown was machine quilted in parallel vertical lines.

3 Trim the excess batting and backing. Use the blue print 2¼"-wide strips to bind the quilt.

TWILIGHT VISIONS

Dusky sashing strips organize the scrappy triangles, which are the stars of this quilt.

Materials

Yardage is based on 42"-wide fabric.

1¼ yards *each* of 2 light blue print shirtings for blocks

2½ yards *total* of assorted medium and dark prints for blocks

½ yard *each* of 5 assorted teal and gray prints for sashing

⅜ yard of red tone on tone for sashing squares

⅝ yard *total* of assorted red prints for border blocks

⅝ yard of light floral print for border blocks

⅝ yard of red print for binding

4⅝ yards of fabric for backing

73" × 83" piece of batting

Cutting

Measurements include ¼"-wide seam allowances.

From *each* of the light blue shirtings, cut:
13 strips, 2⅞" × 42"; crosscut into 168 squares, 2⅞" × 2⅞" (336 total). Cut the squares in half diagonally to make 672 triangles.

From the assorted mediums and darks, cut:
336 squares, 2⅞" × 2⅞"; cut in half diagonally to make 672 triangles

From *each* of the assorted teal and gray prints, cut:
5 strips, 2½" × 42"; crosscut into 20 rectangles, 2½" × 8½" (100 total; 3 are extra)

From the red tone on tone, cut:
4 strips, 2½" × 42"; crosscut into 56 squares, 2½" × 2½"

From the assorted red prints, cut:
69 squares, 2⅞" × 2⅞"; cut in half diagonally to make 138 triangles.

From the light floral print, cut:
6 strips, 2⅞" × 42"; crosscut into 69 squares, 2⅞" × 2⅞". Cut the squares in half diagonally to make 138 triangles.

From the red print for binding, cut:
8 strips, 2¼" × 42"

Cutting Option

If you're not comfortable sewing half-square-triangle units accurately, you can make the 2⅞" squares 3" × 3". After sewing and pressing, trim the units to exactly 2½" square.

CIRCA 1865-1882

Mary Todd Lincoln

Mary Todd Lincoln, who was from a wealthy Kentucky family, had relatives serving the Confederacy, but she supported the work of her husband, Abraham Lincoln, who became president of the United States. She often visited hospitals where wounded soldiers recuperated, and she raised money to help the homeless and refugee slaves in Washington, D.C. However, negative publicity and gossip criticized her frequent shopping sprees and lessened her effectiveness as First Lady. Grief at losing three of her four sons, as well as her husband, led to Lincoln being placed in a mental institution for a time. She challenged the placement and went to live in France before illness forced her return to America.

Making the Blocks

Press the seam allowances as indicated by the arrows in the illustrations.

1 Sew a light print 2⅞" triangle to a medium or dark triangle to make a half-square-triangle unit that measures 2½" square, including seam allowances. Make 672 half-square-triangle units.

Make 672 units,
2½" × 2½".

2 Arrange and sew 16 half-square-triangle units into four rows of four units each. Sew the rows together to complete a block measuring 8½" square, including seam allowances. Make a total of 42 blocks.

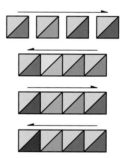 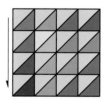

Make 42 blocks,
8½" × 8½".

Assembling and Finishing the Quilt

1 Referring to the quilt assembly diagram on page 58, arrange the blocks in seven rows of six blocks each with the assorted teal and gray print 2½" × 8½" sashing strips in between and at the ends of each row. When you are happy with the block placement, add the red print 2½" sashing squares. Sew the blocks and sashing into rows and sew the sashing and red sashing squares into rows.

2 Sew the block rows and sashing rows together to make the quilt center measuring 62½" × 72½", including seam allowances.

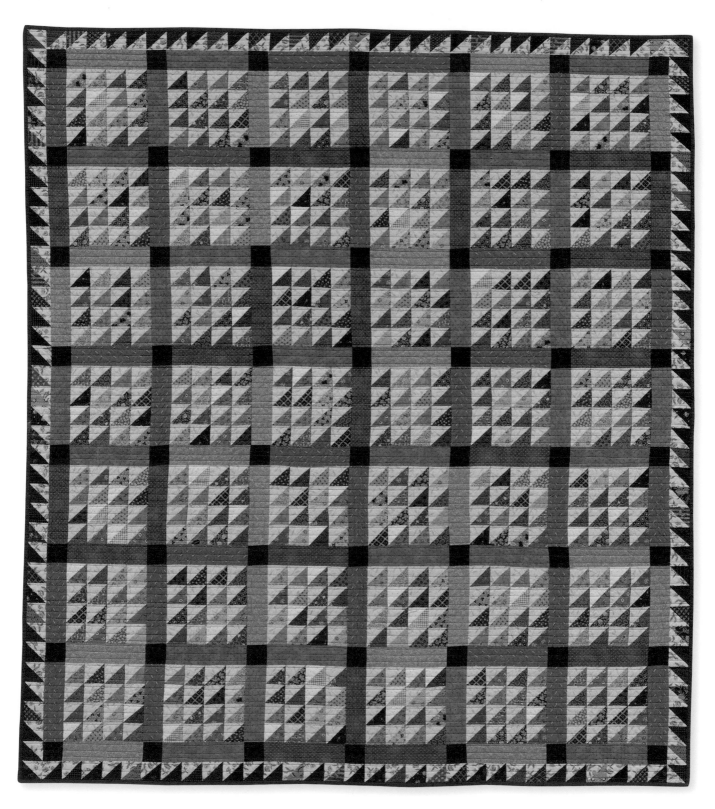

Quilt size: 66½" × 76½" • **Finished block:** 8" × 8"

4 Sew 31 units from step 3 together to make the top/bottom border. Make two borders. Sew 38 units together to make a side border. Make two side borders.

Make 2 top/bottom borders,
2½" × 62½".

Make 2 side borders,
2½" × 76½".

3 Sew a light floral print 2⅞" triangle to an assorted red print triangle to make a half-square-triangle unit measuring 2½" square, including seam allowances. Make 138 units for the border.

Make 138 units,
2½" × 2½".

5 Sew the shorter borders to the top and bottom of the quilt, placing the light triangles adjacent to the quilt center. Sew a longer border to each side of the quilt. The quilt top should measure 66½" × 76½".

6 Layer the backing, batting, and quilt top. Baste, and then quilt as desired. The quilt shown was machine quilted in parallel horizontal lines.

7 Trim the excess batting and backing. Use the red print 2¼"-wide strips to bind the quilt.

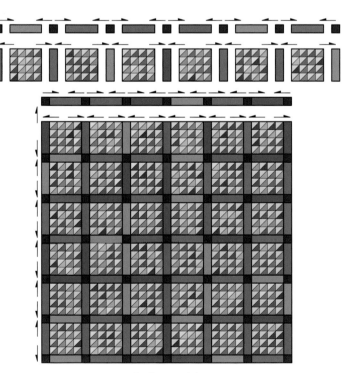

Quilt assembly

The bold, graphic quality of this quilt makes it a fitting tribute to Sojourner Truth.

Materials

Yardage is based on 42"-wide fabric.

2½ yards *total* of assorted light prints for blocks

2¼ yards *total* of assorted medium to dark prints for blocks

1¼ yards *total* of assorted navy prints for blocks

½ yard of red solid for block centers

⅝ yard of navy print for binding

3¼ yards of fabric for backing

58" × 75" piece of batting

Cutting

Measurements include ¼"-wide seam allowances.

Cutting 1 Block

Cut 12 blocks total.

From assorted light prints, cut:

28 squares, 2⅞" × 2⅞"; cut in half diagonally to make 56 triangles

From assorted medium to dark prints, cut:

24 squares, 2⅞" × 2⅞"; cut in half diagonally to make 48 triangles

From assorted navy prints, cut:

6 squares, 4¼" × 4¼"; cut into quarters diagonally to make 24 triangles

From the red solid, cut:

1 square, 6¼" × 6¼"

Cutting the Binding

From the navy print, cut:

7 strips, 2¼" × 42"

Making the Blocks

Press the seam allowances as indicated by the arrows in the illustrations.

1 Sew a light 2⅞" triangle to a dark 2⅞" triangle to make a half-square-triangle unit measuring 2½" square. Make 48 units.

Make 48 units,
2½" × 2½".

2 Arrange and sew half-square-triangle units in rows with two light print 2⅞" triangles and six navy 4¼" triangles as shown. Join the rows together and press to make a side unit. Note that the navy triangles are cut slightly oversized and will be trimmed when the block is complete. Make four side units.

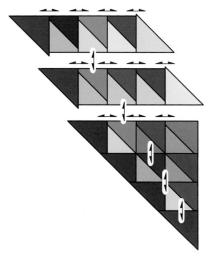

Make 4 side units.

3 Mark the four corner seam intersections on the wrong side of the red 6¼" square. You will sew the side units to the center square with set-in seams.

4 Place a side unit right sides together with the red square, aligning the raw edges and matching the seam intersections. Pin and stitch using a ¼" seam allowance, starting and stopping at the marks and backstitching at each end. Do not stitch into the seam allowance.

Backstitch at each end.

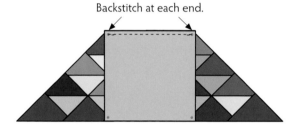

5 Repeat step 4 to sew a side unit to each of the remaining sides of the red square.

6 Fold the block so that the diagonal edges are right sides together; align the raw edges and match the triangle seams, pinning as

CIRCA 1863

Sojourner Truth

African American Sojourner Truth was born a slave named Isabella Baumfree in Ulster County, New York, around 1797. Her first language was the Dutch of her owners. She was bought and sold several times and had four children before she finally escaped to freedom with an infant daughter in 1826, the year before slavery was abolished in the state of New York. As an adult, she changed her name and began lecturing to support the Underground Railroad, universal suffrage, and women's rights. At about six feet tall, she was a mighty force and voice for freedom, and as a runaway slave herself, Sojourner Truth became a powerful speaker for equality.

Quilt size: 51½" × 68½" • **Finished block:** 17" × 17"

Beyond the Battlefield

needed. Sew the seam, beginning at the inside edge, ¼" from the corner of the red square; stitch to the outer corner.

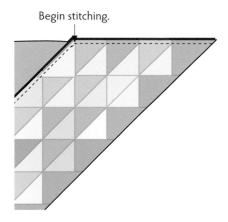

Begin stitching.

7 Repeat step 6 to sew the remaining diagonal seams. Press and trim the block to 17½" square, leaving a ¼" seam allowance beyond the points of the light triangles. Make a total of 12 blocks.

Make 12 blocks,
17½" × 17½".

Assembling and Finishing the Quilt

1 Referring to the quilt assembly diagram at right, arrange the blocks in four rows of three blocks each.

2 To ensure accuracy when joining the blocks, baste them together by machine. Align the raw edges of the first two blocks to be joined. Match all the navy triangles; pin as desired and sew with a long basting stitch. Open up the blocks and check the alignment of the adjacent navy triangles. Fix any unmatched triangles by ripping out the stitches and basting again. When you are happy with the alignment, sew again with a normal stitch length.

3 Repeat step 2 to join the blocks into rows and again when joining the rows. When all rows have been sewn together, the quilt top should measure 51½" × 68½".

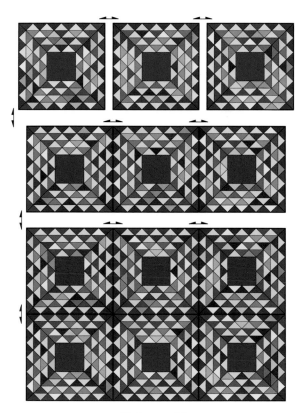

Quilt assembly

4 Layer the backing, batting, and quilt top. Baste, and then quilt as desired. The quilt shown was machine quilted in parallel horizontal lines.

5 Trim the excess batting and backing. Use the navy print 2¼"-wide strips to bind the quilt.

BEST OF ALL

Can you believe this quilt is made from just one block? It almost looks like a sampler quilt due to the changing placement of colors and values. We love disappearing blocks and try to include one in each quilt that we make.

Materials

Yardage is based on 42"-wide fabric.

4¼ yards *total* of assorted prints in blue, red, green, brown, gray, gold, black, and teal for blocks
1¼ yards of dark brown print for sashing
¼ yard of red print for sashing cornerstones
⅝ yard of dark brown print for binding
3⅝ yards of fabric for backing
65" × 65" piece of batting

Cutting

Refer to "Disappearing Blocks" on page 66 before you cut. Measurements include ¼"-wide seam allowances.

Cutting 1 Block

Cut 16 total.

From the print for piece A, cut:
1 square, 4½" × 4½"

From the print for piece B, cut:
4 squares, 2⅞" × 2⅞"; cut in half diagonally to make 8 triangles

From the print for piece C, cut:
4 squares, 1¹⁵⁄₁₆" × 1¹⁵⁄₁₆"*

* To cut this odd size, align your ruler exactly halfway between the 1⅞" and 2" lines.

From the print for piece D, cut:
2 squares, 3¼" × 3¼"; cut in quarters diagonally to make 8 triangles

From the print for piece E, cut:
4 squares, 2½" × 2½"

From the print for piece F, cut:
8 squares, 2⅞" × 2⅞"; cut in half diagonally to make 16 triangles**

From the print for piece G, cut:
8 squares, 2⅞" × 2⅞"; cut in half diagonally to make 16 triangles**

** These are for the half-square-triangle units and should have some contrast with each other.

From the print for piece H, cut:
4 squares, 2½" × 2½"

Cutting the Sashing and Binding

From dark brown print for sashing, cut:
3 strips, 12½" × 42"; crosscut into 40 rectangles, 2½" × 12½"

From the red print, cut:
2 strips, 2½" × 42"; crosscut into 25 squares, 2½" × 2½"

From dark brown print for binding, cut:
7 strips, 2¼" × 42"

CIRCA 1855-1865

"Belle" Boyd

Born in the North, Virginian Maria Isabelle "Belle" Boyd became a spy for the Confederacy. She was arrested several times and even continued sending messages from prison in Washington, D.C., by putting her notes in rubber balls and bouncing them outside to a waiting helper or by rolling information around marbles. Boyd used her charm to deceive officers and obtain information. She often put herself in danger, and when captured, vowed never to break down. After the war, she became an actress in London, and later, wrote and sold her colorful memoirs.

Disappearing Blocks

We define a disappearing block as one that takes on a different appearance from the primary block, created simply with the magic of fabric placement and color choices. These blocks might look like a mistake, but they make a quilt so much more interesting.

Because the blocks in our quilt are scrappy and the placement of colors and values within the blocks varies, refer to the piece letters in the block diagrams as a guide for choosing fabrics. Be creative and study the blocks in the quilt photo on page 67 to choose colors and values for various pieces of the blocks.

Depending on fabric choices, the stars in the block centers can be prominent, look like a flower, or disappear altogether. See if you can spot the renegade block and have fun coming up with your own disappearing blocks!

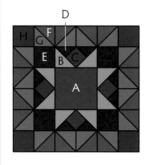 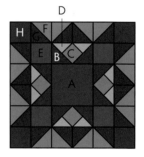

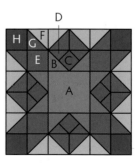

Block shading options

Quilt size: 58½" × 58½" • **Finished block:** 12" × 12"

Making the Blocks

Press the seam allowances as indicated by the arrows in the illustrations.

1 Sew a 3¼" triangle for piece D to one side of a 1¹⁵⁄₁₆" C square. Sew a second triangle to the adjacent side. Make four units.

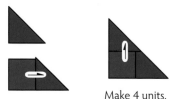

Make 4 units.

2 Sew a 2⅞" triangle for piece B to each of the remaining sides of the square to make a pieced rectangle that measures 2½" × 4½", including seam allowances. Make four units.

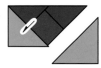

Make 4 units,
2½" × 4½".

3 Sew a 2⅞" F triangle to a contrasting 2⅞" G triangle to make a half-square-triangle unit that measures 2½" square, including seam allowances. Make 16 units.

Make 16 units,
2½" × 2½".

4 Sew four half-square-triangle units together to make the side of the block. Make four block sides that measure 2½" × 8½", including seam allowances.

Make 4 units,
2½" × 8½".

5 Arrange and sew the units from step 2, the four 2½" squares for piece E, and the dark 4½" A square in three rows as shown. Sew the rows together to complete the block center, which should measure 8½" square, including seam allowances.

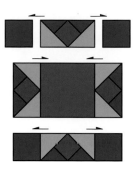
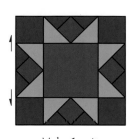

Make 1 unit,
8½" × 8½".

6 Sew two units from step 4 to the sides of the block center. Add the four 2½" squares for piece H to the ends of the remaining two side units and sew these to the top and bottom to complete the block. It should measure 12½" square, including seam allowances. Make 16 blocks.

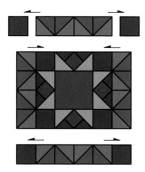
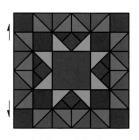

Make 16 blocks,
12½" × 12½".

Going Rogue

If you look closely at our quilt, you'll notice that there's a rogue or renegade block in the bottom row. The half-square-triangle units around the outer edges of the block were rotated to create yet another look.

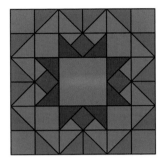

Renegade block

Assembling and Finishing the Quilt

1 Arrange the blocks in four rows of four blocks each. Place the dark brown 2½" × 12½" sashing strips between the blocks and at the end of each row. Sew the blocks and sashing strips into rows. Make four rows that measure 12½" × 58½", including seam allowances.

Make 4 rows,
12½" × 58½".

2 Sew four brown 2½" × 12½" sashing strips together with five red print 2½" sashing cornerstones as shown to make the sashing row. Make five rows that measure 2½" × 58½", including seam allowances.

Make 5 rows,
2½" × 58½".

3 Sew the rows together, alternating the sashing rows and block rows as shown in the quilt assembly diagram. The quilt top should measure 58½" square.

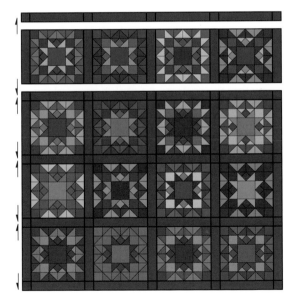

Quilt assembly

4 Layer the backing, batting, and quilt top. Baste, and then quilt as desired. The quilt shown was quilted by Sue Urich in an overall Baptist fan design.

5 Trim the excess batting and backing. Use the dark brown print 2¼"-wide strips to bind the quilt.

STITCHING A LIFE

It's interesting how wide triangles mimic the look of gentle curves from afar.

Quilt size: 31" × 39½" • **Finished block:** 6" × 6"

Materials

Yardage is based on 42"-wide fabric.

12 pieces, 4" × 10", of assorted light prints for blocks
¾ yard *total* of assorted medium to dark prints
12 pieces, 5" × 5", of assorted tan prints for blocks
1⅓ yards of light floral print for setting blocks, outer border, and binding
¼ yard of dark floral print for inner border
1⅓ yards of fabric for backing
37" × 46" piece of batting
Freezer paper for templates

Cutting

See "Using Freezer-Paper Templates" at right. Measurements include ¼"-wide seam allowances.

From *each* of the light prints, cut:
8 triangles using A (96 total)

From the assorted medium and dark prints, cut:
12 sets of 16 matching triangles:
 • 8 using B (96 total)
 • 8 using C (96 total)
12 sets of 4 matching squares, 2½" × 2½" (48 total)
12 sets of 4 matching squares, 1¼" × 1¼" (48 total)
12 squares, 1" × 1"*

Some of these squares for the block centers match the outer 1¼" squares, while others don't. It's your choice!

Continued on page 72

Using Freezer-Paper Templates

1. Trace the template patterns on page 73 onto the paper side of the freezer paper and cut out the shapes on the drawn lines.

2. Iron the freezer-paper templates, shiny side down, onto the right side of the chosen light and dark fabrics.

3. Cut ¼" beyond the freezer-paper templates with a rotary cutter and ruler.

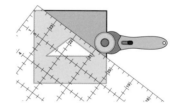

4. With the freezer paper still in place, sew the pieces together, matching points, to make a flying-geese unit.

5. Remove the freezer paper and press. You can reuse the freezer paper as long as it continues to adhere to the fabric. Cut new pieces as needed.

CIRCA 1868

Elizabeth Keckley

Elizabeth Keckley, a former slave, bought her freedom and set up a dressmaking business in the nation's capital city. Two of her customers were the wives of Jefferson Davis and Robert E. Lee. In 1861, she made a dress for Mary Todd Lincoln, and the two women became close friends until 1868, when Keckley published a memoir and included details about Mrs. Lincoln. Always willing to help others, Keckley created an organization that worked to help runaway slaves find food, places to live, and work. She ran a successful business, but Keckley is still best known as Mrs. Lincoln's dressmaker.

Continued from page 70

From *each* of the tan prints, cut:
4 rectangles, 1" × 3¼" (48 total)

From the light floral print, cut:
6 squares, 6½" × 6½"
3 squares, 10" × 10"; cut into quarters diagonally
    to make 12 triangles (2 are extra)
2 squares, 6" × 6"; cut in half diagonally to make
    4 triangles
4 strips, 2½" × 42"; crosscut into:
  • 2 strips, 2½" × 27"
  • 2 strips, 2½" × 39½"
4 strips, 2¼" × 42"*

Or cut enough bias strips to make 154" of binding.

From the dark floral print, cut:
4 strips, 1" × 42"; crosscut into:
  • 2 strips, 1" × 26"
  • 2 strips, 1" × 35½"

Making the Blocks

Press the seam allowances as indicated by the arrows in the illustrations.

1 Referring to "Using Freezer-Paper Templates" on page 70, and using triangles cut from a light print and a dark print, make eight flying-geese units measuring 2½" × 1¼", including seam allowances.

Make 8 units,
2½" × 1¼".

2 Arrange and sew two flying-geese units, one 1¼" square, and one 2½" square as shown to make a corner unit measuring 3¼" square, including seam allowances. Make four units.

Make 4 units,
3¼" × 3¼".

3 Arrange and sew the units from step 2 together with four 1" × 3¼" rectangles and one 1" square as shown to complete the block. It should measure 6½" square, including seam allowances. Make a total of 12 blocks.

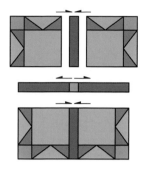 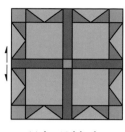

Make 12 blocks,
6½" × 6½".

Assembling and Finishing the Quilt

1 Arrange the blocks, light floral setting squares, and light floral triangles in diagonal rows. Sew the blocks and triangles into rows. Sew the rows together and add the corner triangles.

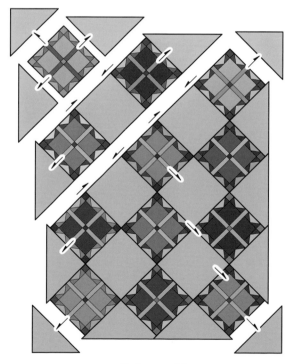

Quilt assembly

2 Trim and square up the quilt to measure 26" × 34½", making sure there is at least

¼" seam allowance beyond the points of the blocks.

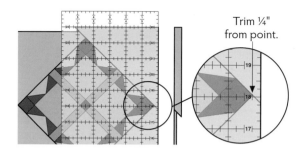

Trim ¼"
from point.

3 Add a dark floral print 1" × 26" strip to the top and bottom of the quilt. Then add a dark floral 1" × 35½" strip to each side.

4 Add a light print 2½" × 27" strip to the top and bottom of the quilt. Add a 2½" × 39½" strip to each side. The quilt top should now measure 31" × 39½".

5 Layer the backing, batting, and quilt top. Baste, and then quilt as desired. The quilt shown was machine quilted in an overall meandering pattern.

6 Trim the excess batting and backing. We chose to round the corners of our quilt. To do this, position a 5"-diameter plate or cardboard circle at the corner and trace the curve. Trim the corner on the drawn line.

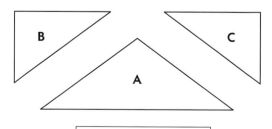

Trim.

5"

7 Use the light floral print 2¼"-wide strips to bind the quilt.

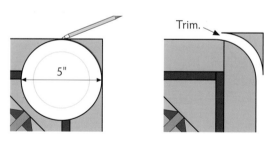

B   C

A

Patterns do not include
seam allowances.

This antique quilt is spectacular in both its simplicity and its sheer number of fabrics.

Materials

Yardage is based on 42"-wide fabric.

3½ yards *total* of assorted medium and dark prints for blocks

2⅝ yards *total* of assorted light prints for blocks

½ yard of medium print for binding

3¼ yards of fabric for backing

57" × 62" piece of batting

Ruler with 45° angle line or template material

Cutting

Measurements include ¼"-wide seam allowances.

Cutting 1 Block

Cut 110 blocks total.

From the assorted medium and dark prints, cut:
2 sets of 4 matching 1½" 45° diamonds*

From the assorted light prints, cut:
4 matching squares, 2" × 2"
1 square, 3¼" × 3¼"; cut into quarters diagonally to make 4 triangles

Cutting the Binding

From the medium print, cut:
6 strips, 2¼" × 42"

Cut the diamonds using a template made from the pattern on page 79 or with your rotary cutter and ruler, following the instructions in "Cutting 45° Diamonds" at right.

Cutting 45° Diamonds

For each diamond, you'll need a 1½" × 4" rectangle. A 1½" × 12" strip will yield four matching diamonds.

1. Align the 45° line of a rotary ruler with the bottom edge of the 1½" × 12" strip and cut the corner off the strip.

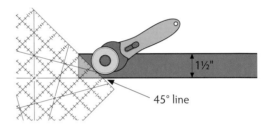

45° line

2. Slide the ruler over to align the 1½" line of the ruler with the cut edge of the fabric. Cut along the right edge of the ruler to make one diamond. Cut four matching diamonds. You'll need two sets of four matching diamonds (eight total) for each LeMoyne Star block.

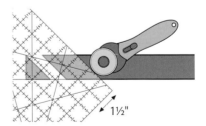

Cut 4 matching diamonds.

CIRCA 1868

Harriet Tubman

Harriet Tubman, originally a slave in Maryland named Araminta "Minty" Ross, escaped to Philadelphia as a young woman in 1849. Tubman subsequently led over three hundred slaves northward to freedom and became known as "Moses," the most famous conductor of the Underground Railroad. Tubman also worked as a scout, spy, and nurse, but she was denied a pension for wartime services. She did receive one as her veteran husband's widow. She died in 1913. Tubman was the first African American woman honored with her image on a United States postage stamp. March 10 has been designated as Harriet Tubman Day.

Making the Blocks

Press the seam allowances as indicated by the arrows in the illustrations.

1 Choose two sets of four matching diamonds for one block. (Note that some blocks include more than two fabrics; feel free to improvise and make do as the original quilter did.) Place one of each of the diamonds right sides together with raw edges aligned. Begin sewing at the sharp point and sew until you are ¼" away from the next point; stop sewing and backstitch two or three stitches before removing the unit from the machine. Make four pairs.

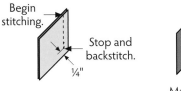

Make 4 pairs.

2 Sew two pairs together in the same manner to make a half block. Make two half blocks. Press seam allowances so that they are all going the same direction.

Make 2 units.

3 Align the two half blocks, matching the centers. Pin as desired and sew the halves together, starting and stopping ¼" from the outer edges on each side.

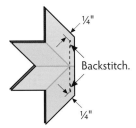

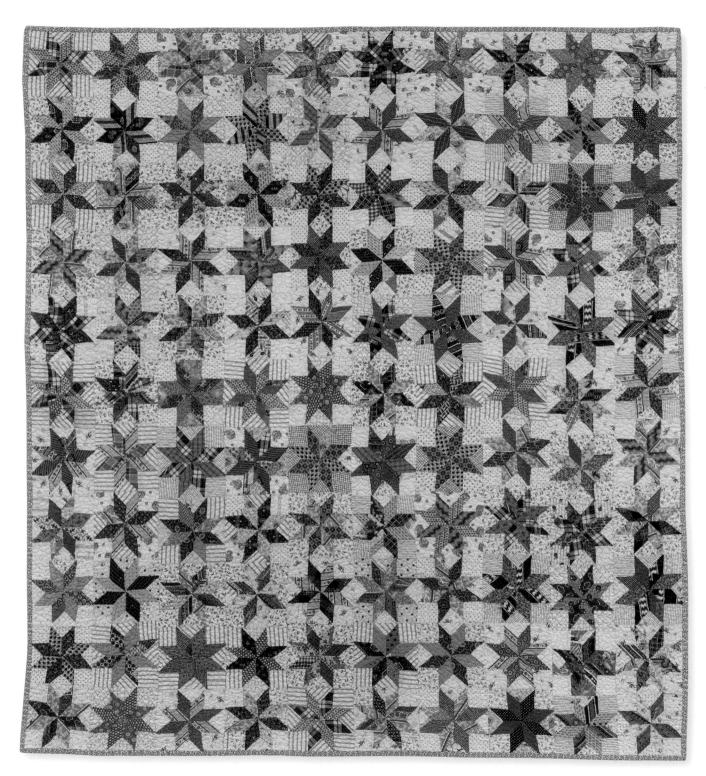

Quilt size: 50½" × 55½" • **Finished block:** 5" × 5"

North Star

4 Arrange four matching triangles around the star with all the fabrics right side up. Pick up the star and one triangle, aligning the side of the triangle with the adjacent diamond, right sides together. Align the outer points and insert a couple of pins to keep the pieces in place. With the diamond on top, sew from the outer point toward the star center. Fold the next diamond and seam allowance out of the way as you near the center. Stop sewing a few threads away from the ¼" seam intersection and backstitch. Remove the unit from the machine.

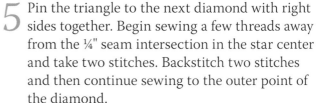

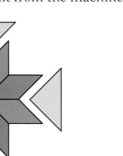

Backstitch.

¼"

5 Pin the triangle to the next diamond with right sides together. Begin sewing a few threads away from the ¼" seam intersection in the star center and take two stitches. Backstitch two stitches and then continue sewing to the outer point of the diamond.

6 Check the set-in seam and if you are satisfied with it, press the seam allowances toward the triangle. Repeat the procedure to add the remaining three triangles.

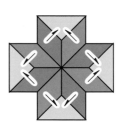

7 Add the corner squares in a similar manner, pinning so that the outer edge of the square aligns with the outer edge of the triangle. Sew one edge at a time, starting on the outer edge of the block for the first seam and then at the star center for the second seam, as you did for the triangles.

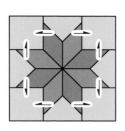

8 After adding the four corner squares, the block should measure 5½" square, including seam allowances. Make a total of 110 blocks.

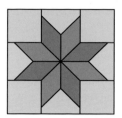

Make 110 blocks,
5½" × 5½".

Assembling and Finishing the Quilt

1 Referring to the quilt assembly diagram below, arrange and sew the blocks in 11 rows of 10 blocks each. Sew the rows together to complete the quilt top, which should measure 50½" × 55½".

2 Layer the backing, batting, and quilt top. Baste, and then quilt as desired. The antique quilt shown was recently assembled and machine quilted in an overall meandering pattern.

3 Trim the excess batting and backing. Use the medium print 2¼"-wide strips to bind the quilt.

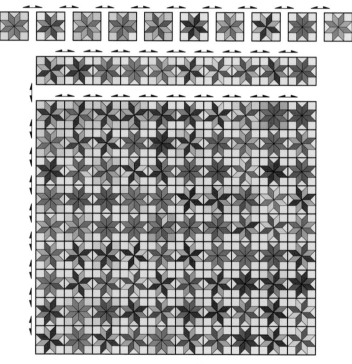

Quilt assembly

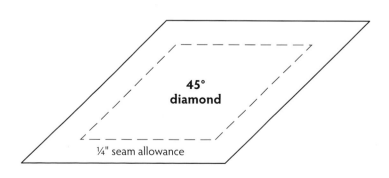

45°
diamond

¼" seam allowance

Mary (*right*) and Connie (*left*) talk nearly every day and remain best friends. Both have serious fabric addictions, and they both still LOVE making quilts! Visit them at www.country-threads-chicken-scratch.com.

Connie Tesene

I started quilting in America's bicentennial year, 1976, and have seen many changes in the quilt industry since then. My first quilt was made with templates cut from cardboard, traced around with a pencil, and cut out with scissors. The rotary cutter hadn't even been invented yet! Wow, times have certainly changed for the better!

Since closing the quilt shop in 2014, I've enjoyed the luxury of time—time for gardening, babysitting, dog walking, volunteering, traveling, reading, and, of course, quiltmaking. My husband, Roy, and I still live in the home where we raised our three boys. It's a wonderful house with an extended garden, but the house is also 120 years old, so it's always in need of work. The gardens look great when you drive by, but don't get too close or you'll see the weeds!

I would like to be remembered as a maker of pies, quilts, gardens, art, fun, and a cozy home.

Mary Etherington

Like Connie, I made my first quilt in 1976 with a cardboard template and scissors. When the rotary cutter came along, our quilting lives changed for the better.

Rick and I still live on the Country Threads farm with goats, geese, fancy chickens, dogs, cats, and two parakeets. I'll be taking care of animals the rest of my life!

I've been a church pianist off and on for 60 years now, and play for services and the choir almost every Sunday. I love reading, caring for my extensive collection of cacti and succulents, and quiltmaking.

My number one cause is animal welfare, and I pray that puppy mills become extinct in my lifetime. There's nothing more disturbing to me than animal neglect and abuse that goes unpunished.